Humble Work & Mad Wanderings

STREET LIFE IN THE MACHINE AGE

❧

Ken Appollo

CARL MAUTZ PUBLISHING

NEVADA CITY 1997

To outdoor work and daydreams,
my father and mother and May.

CONTENTS

WHEN I was old enough to count money and make change, my grand-father let me tend his small roadside vegetable stand. To my amazement, people stopped their cars and freely paid for tomatoes, corn and other things grown in the backyard. Years later, I was inspired to sit behind a beautiful chalk drawing on pavement recently abandoned by a street artist. Before it an encircled "Merci" invited contributions. The site of this public exhibition was the unrenovated Pont des Arts, a walking bridge over the Seine. I sat there in the heart of old Paris facing Pont Neuf and Notre Dame. The Louvre was to my left and the Eiffel Tower and a setting sun were behind me. I was homeless and broke and sur-rounded by beauty. I felt grateful and my thoughts wandered freely, interrupted only by the sounds of coins dropped before me and polite snapshot requests. Thus newfound patrons surprised me repeatedly, as if exchanging gold for fresh toma-toes. I had survived another day on the street.

Posing for tourists is humble work, but not long ago, a working man was lucky if he owned the clothes on his back and a good pair of shoes. In Europe and America, the Industrial Revolution changed the way most people worked and organized their lives. It raised expectations and sold a lot of clocks and watches. It also called attention to the kinds of work that sustained those least affected by these changes—the lowly. Poor street sellers survived on the edges of the Industrial Age. Whether they offered flowers or candy to people passing by, their appeal was immediate and ancient. By the end of the nineteenth century, public commerce of this type would be controversial. Meanwhile industry put people on the street. With factories booming, more workers were recruited than were needed, stranding the unemployed. Often early industrial work was seasonal or otherwise deter-mined by demand. Layoffs were common. For other reasons, not everyone was suited for factory work and if you were injured working, you could lose your job. In the absence of workmen's compensation, unemployment benefits and welfare, street occupations formed a time-tested safety net that caught the unemployed. Its notable eccentricities aside, the street provided a conservative setting for people who needed to regroup and recover. It attracted individuals who welcomed the slow pace of subsistence work.

Many privileged Victorians saw the poorer classes in a romantic light. Idealizing the poor was a way of dealing with their growing numbers, but there was one overriding reason for upperclass denial and attentiveness: anyone might end up down on their luck. Industrialization frightened people as surely as it uplifted them.

If some Victorians romanticized the lowly, others criminalized them. After the mid-nineteenth century, it became more difficult to work along European and American streets. Pushcart use was increasingly restricted. New laws made beggars of wandering musicians. Permits and licenses were used to regulate and discourage street workers. Some traditional occupations were banned outright, but it was finally motorized vehicles that overran the streets and crowded the sidewalks, changing cities as nothing short of warfare ever had. The world was losing its innocents.

Ironically, modern failures at keeping peace and banishing poverty have kept street life alive. Sociologists decided that street workers are good for cities after all. They help define neighborhoods, draw people outside, provide watchful eyes upon the street and so on.*

Others questioned how much one hundred years of technological change has improved upon thousands of years of evolving city life. Moreover, what was once bothersome was now nostalgic. An American revival of street life, born of economic necessity, sanctioned by social scientists and shouted by hippies, began in the 1960s.

A decade earlier, before I was aware of sociology, I was growing up in a New Jersey suburb on the rise that was looking less and less ethnic. The little old ladies who dressed in black and spoke only Italian, the ones my mother said came over on the same boat as my grandmother, were disappearing. The coming blandness of the suburbs, informed by *National Geographic* and *Life* magazines, took me elsewhere. In 1956, at age eight, I purchased a ten cent lot of unmounted cabinet photographs at a St. Vincent de Paul rummage sale. Tied by a miniature green portfolio, the lot featured romantic portraits of Italian peasants. This artistic turn in my childhood put me on my present course and for all my collecting detours in the years since then, my acquisitions have been modest. I can fit most of my street life collection in an overnight suitcase.

I arrived at this compact result by first passing over lithographs of the working poor. They were expensive and idealized. Photographs were less veiled, and the first snapshots were silent revolutionaries, belonging to the millions. My early photograph hunting involved more looking than buying. I browsed bookstores and galleries in the late 1960s when photography enjoyed renewed popularity. I was impressed by the street photography of John Thomson, Eugene Atget, Jacob Riis and Lewis Hine, but their masterworks were beyond my means. I wanted to get to the heart of the matter, so I collected images from family sources: cased miniatures, card mounted photographs, stereoviews, post cards, snapshots and other small format keepsakes.

I favored the most basic varieties of employment, collecting photographs of individuals who were able to drag, carry or push something onto the street that made them a living. I ignored the peddler and his wagon as too prosperous, and lamplighters, town criers and other city employees as too secure.

I was drawn to photographs of the working poor in transition—wandering, falling, ascending. So far as I know, my immigrant grandparents never pushed carts hawking fresh fruit. My Italian grandmother first sewed piecework in a Manhattan tenement. The men in her family worked in factories and stone quarries. All the same, there was an elaborate system of street work available to those who needed it.

What finally distinguishes street work from other poor labor is its prehistoric roots. In its simple, seasonal and wandering aspects, it recalls hunting and gathering. It is independent of motorized vehicles, computers, formal education and all other accessories to modern employment. It is the direct, uncomplicated nature of this work that puts it at odds with the post-industrial world.

What of places where industrialization has yet to occur or is less advanced than in the West? My thoughts about street life were influenced by a trip to Mainland China in 1980. I went to China as a tourist, expecting its citizens to be either peasants or factory workers. To my surprise, the streets were filled with street traders. My enthusiasm for photographing street life made one of my tour guides uncomfortable. To him this subject matter was unflattering. At his suggestion I took a snapshot of a newly constructed concrete municipal building and thereafter documented street workers with greater discretion.

Modernization can be uplifting at first, but it tends toward standardization. One toy store in a mall has the same toys, arranged in the same way, as the toy store in the next mall. The street is less regimented. When street life dies, so dies part of the human body and spirit. Extinction of our species need not come from above like an atom bomb or the greenhouse effect. It may come one small defeat at a time.

The sampling of photographs that follows is an occupational primer. In the street, work is reduced to its most basic elements. Among these randomly collected images, the organ grinder is featured. Developed before industrial times, the barrel organ inspired and extended the bounds of mechanical music. The organ grinder was essentially a human jukebox. The player piano, phonograph, radio and all subsequent forms of canned music are his descendants. Looking backwards, minstrels, animal trainers and wandering entertainers of every possible description preceded him.

The beautiful handcrafted barrel organ was reinvented in the Machine Age. Less rare and curious, even when lacking inlaid, painted and automaton embellishments, it never became as standardized as the Edison phonograph. Still, John Thomson may have excluded the organ grinder from his classic photographic study, *Street Life in London* (1877–78), as too common. Popular estimates counted thousands of organ grinders in Thomson's London. By the time Atget photographed his organ grinder a few decades later, the minstrel mechanic had become a vanishing symbol of the past.

Curiously enough, the earliest known photograph of a human being, a fuzzy detail of Daguerre's 1839 view of Boulevard du Temple, depicts another common street scene, a bootblack working on a gentleman's shoe. But this book is not meant to be an exhaustive study of Victorian street life in photographs. Many rare and beautiful examples of this genre have been collected and published elsewhere. It is not my intention to duplicate these efforts. Rather I have assembled a group of images and occupations that reflect my personal understanding and experience of the subject. I regret that I cannot include images in my mind's eye or those missed, lost or still sought. One of these mental snapshots is of a blind man playing a tin flute, huddled in ragged blankets on a wintry Parisian street. The tune he played was his own composition and he was assisted by a small dog that danced on its hind legs. I passed this pair in a handful of heartbeats over twenty years ago and miraculously, they are still with me.

What else can be said of street life where it survives? It speaks of human ingenuity and tenacity and the varieties of human employment. In the images that follow, style and content sometimes clash, a consequence of being poor and photographed. Some of the photographs are attended by personal anecdotes. I included these stories for the same reason that a doctor hangs his diplomas in the outer office: to make the guess-work more credible.

*Jane Jacobs, *The Death and Life of Great American Cities*, Random House, New York, 1961, p. 35.

I once hitchhiked everywhere,
wrote poems between rides,
and never heard the distant guns.
Innocent before work and war,
lost youth, forgive my wanderings.

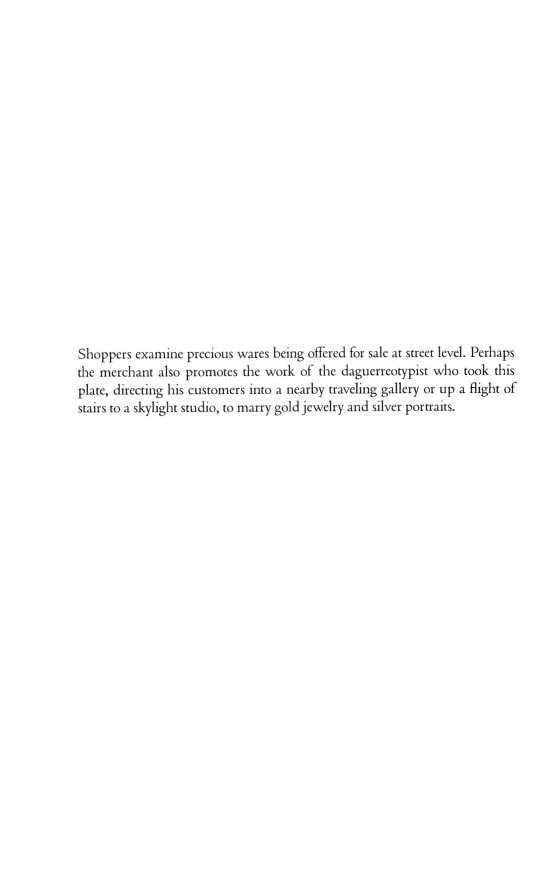

Shoppers examine precious wares being offered for sale at street level. Perhaps the merchant also promotes the work of the daguerreotypist who took this plate, directing his customers into a nearby traveling gallery or up a flight of stairs to a skylight studio, to marry gold jewelry and silver portraits.

1. JEWELRY VENDOR. *Anonymous sixth plate daguerreotype, c. 1855, found sealed atypically with wax in the style of portraits set in jewelry. Courtesy of Barbara Isenburg.*

2. THE WALKING AGENT. *Carte de visite by D. M. Fulton of Lancaster, Ohio.*
No. 2 of a series, the "Walking Picture, 61,117 miles to January 22nd, 1873."

3. THE OLD LEATHERMAN. *Anonymous cabinet card, c. 1880s.*

I missed an opportunity to buy this rare photograph in 1972, because I was confused by the woman's dress. We have come to think of street laborers as lowlife. It wasn't long ago that a street occupation was just another job. In the 1850s, American street workers were less numerous, more appreciated and less regulated than the workers who followed them. Except for the poorest workers, men wore ties and jackets and women wore proper dresses. By the end of the nineteenth century a more ragged look would be commonplace, a change of fashion consistent with the changing times.

4. BOOK VENDING CRONE. *Anonymous sixth plate ambrotype, c. 1856. Courtesy of Herb Peck.*

5. POPCORN VENDOR. *Anonymous sixth plate ambrotype, c. late 1850s.*

6. NEW TEAPOTS, OLD CLOTHES. *Anonymous quarter plate tintype, c. 1860.*

7. Sticks of equal length. *Carte de visite by Gardner, Washington, D.C., c. late 1860s.*

8. CANDY SAM. *Mounted albumen photograph from an 1867 Yale University class album.*

9. THE YANKEE DOODLE WHISTLER. *Carte de visite published by T. R. Burnham, 1869.*
A street cobbler and a well-known Boston character. His whistling was his cry.

10. FISH SELLER. *Carte de visite, c. 1860s. "Zebeder the fisherman of Stonington, Connecticut a village character" in pencil reverse.*

"Altogether it will be seen that the commons and open spaces in and about London, are not merely useful in maintaining the health of the population, and as affording some space of recreation; but they also open out new fields of industry for those who earn their living out of doors."

–JOHN THOMSON, *Street Life in London*, 1876.
"Chapham Common Industries" by Adolphe Smith.

11. DONKEY FOR HIRE. *Anonymous French stereoview, c. 1860.*

12. ARAB BEGGARS. *Carte de visite by Alary and Geiser, Alger, "Mendiants, 1864" in pencil reverse.*

I KNOW from personal experience that begging is a form of work, perhaps not the most productive or evolved activity, but work and hard work just the same. The two Arabs in plate 12 are professional beggars. A person is hungry and scared before he is ragged, but if he is to be believed, he'd best look the part.

I was once hungry enough to ask strangers for money. It took hours to find the courage to ask the first person and repeated rejections and delays to secure enough change for a meal. You may grant that this activity is difficult and mortifying, but how is it useful? What commodity or service does the beggar provide? Personally, I rarely give a beggar money, but I have never walked by one without feeling guilty, lucky or otherwise self-examined—this is the service that worker provides. A beggar is a mirror: he is paid to protest.

When I panhandled, I gave up asking for money for food because that kind of truth makes strangers uncomfortable. I discovered that it was less traumatic and more profitable to ask for money to see a movie. This lateral career change was suggested by a line of my longhaired peers queuing to see the movie *Easy Rider* at a Paris Latin Quarter theater. What had taken painful hours now took minutes. The only drawback to this approach is that I was sometimes given what I asked for, a movie ticket. Before seeing *Easy Rider* twenty times, I found another way to survive.

Begging can be further explained by a riddle that Abraham Lincoln liked to tell. It goes, how many legs does a dog have if you call a tail a leg? "Five" is the common response, but the correct answer is "four"—calling a tail a leg doesn't make it a leg. Historically street performers have been classified as beggars to demean or diminish them. That kind of beggar is a five-legged dog. Like I said, I don't usually give money to beggars, but it would never occur to me to outlaw them. Society's judgement over time has been harsher. They have been sent to work houses, jails and asylums. They have been prayed over and they have hurt other street workers by association, for the street poor, whatever they do, appear as beggars. Working outdoors in humbling conditions, they beg for your business. An accumulated mass of laws ought to insulate the modern pedestrian from the poor at street level, but it doesn't. As other street workers are restricted and outmoded, beggars grow more visible and aggressive.

13. Onions by the bunch. *Carte de visite by Merille, Mexico City, c. 1860s.*

Christiano Junior.

14. BIRD SELLER. *Carte de visite by Christiano Junior, Rio de Janeiro, c. 1860s. In a perfect world, one would only be allowed to sell as many parrots as he could carry.*

16. YOUNG THIEF. *Carte de visite by Ritter, Molkenteller & Co.,
Bombay and Poona, India. "Young Thief" in ink, album I.D., 1870.*

FROM the early days of forming this collection, I decided to exclude images of criminals and their subculture. That raised questions about what constituted criminal and noncriminal activities. Is the beggar a criminal because he is annoying? Prostitutes are criminals in some places and not others, so their crimes are not universal. And even though the thief is widely despised, the person who steals food because he is hungry is sometimes forgiven.

In plate 16 a young thief is overshadowed by two large policemen. This small studio photograph approximates an arrest—I include it because it reminds me of one of my own.

I was young and in love and in Paris. Unfortunately the woman I loved was in New York. I was trying to misspend my youth in the best way possible, but I was also broke and homeless, so not all my youthful memories are romantic. For example, how can I exorcise the hard-hitting police who trespass my imagination?

In the spring of 1970, while visiting a merchant marine friend and his fifteen-year-old son one evening, our conversation was interrupted by shouting in the street below us. Looking out a window we saw a bedraggled, jeering group of protesters before an advancing formation of riot police. When the police march changed to double-time, the protesters exited from our view in full retreat. This vignette was puzzling and the police, with their clear plastic helmets and shields, seemed so out of place in the Paris night that the son and I went out in search of an explanation. His French was good and we soon understood what we had seen. A previously illegal right wing group was having its first public meeting and the police were there to protect them from objecting leftists.

The protesters were regrouping nearby on boulevard St. Germain, so we made our way there. We stood among them blocking traffic. Suddenly, a line of riot police moved up the boulevard in our direction. A student leader shouted instructions. I hesitated, not understanding his French. My companion was gone, taken away by the fleeing crowd. I turned too slowly up rue St. Jacques. Across the street I noticed a girl, a street junkie known in that quarter. Riot policemen were charging up and down St. Jacques. Since I had nowhere to run, I sat down on the curb and covered my head as best I could. I wasn't beaten so much as whipped by clubs made of flexible hard rubber. Across the street I heard the cries of the girl, pitifully under-medicated for the moment. The peace-keepers had captured one short, stoned female and an English-speaking refugee. What came next is more troubling.

The shielded cops dropped me inside the entrance of a paddy wagon the size of a bus. The bus driver silently looked down on me. I told him scornfully that I didn't speak French. He responded by pulling a sap out of somewhere and raising a welt on the back of the hand that grasped the support railing above me. I looked at my hand and stared at him. Someone from the back of the bus came forward, attempting to cool me, telling me kindly in English that it would be best if I took a seat. I don't know how many times I've relived the scene with the bus driver. I relive it now; straight-arming his head through the window behind him, I open the door and make my escape. I would rather not relive this moment down the years.

The next part of this roundup consisted of being taken to the nearby Pantheon police station. The cells were already filled when I arrived and so too were the benches by the front desk. I was confused by what I saw. It was explained to me that in the event of an illegal manifestation, it was against the law to be on the street. Most of the people in the holding cell looked as if their Saturday night dates had been interrupted. I looked as if I had been beaten and rolled on the ground. In short, I looked guilty and the French had just passed a tough outside agitator law. It provided foreigners caught participating in illegal demonstrations with mandatory two year jail sentences. I found a student who spoke English and told him a story about having been in a car accident recently. I suspected that the police had reinjured my head. He went up to the front desk and ran this yarn by a skeptical officer. The student came back and said that I would have to faint. I saw the genius of his plan in a instant, but I wasn't sure that I could go through with it. As he began clearing a bench for me, I sat down and put my head between my knees. Next thing I knew I was being helped down, eyes closed, and new allies were making a convincing spontaneous display of the martyr to police brutality before them. A stretcher arrived shortly and I was transported outside into the cool night air.

I was carried into a waiting paddy wagon. Once inside, doors closed, I realized that I was in a small dark room surrounded by hostile cops. The stretcher was banged around a little and there were side-comments. The most easily understood was "publicité." They clearly didn't find my performance convincing. I kept my eyes closed all the way to the hospital. There I was examined by a sympathetic medical team and an old lady gave me a delousing, which I didn't need or appreciate. Finally I was pushed across a cobblestone courtyard in something resembling a wheelbarrow to a waiting bed.

My first day in the hospital I called the American Embassy and logged a complaint. The second day a police detective visited and suggested that I voluntarily come by the police station afterwards to talk about what I was doing in France and how long I planned to be doing it. That never happened. Released the next day, I walked to American Express to check my mail. To my surprise a lone national policeman guarded the entrance with a machine gun. As he looked me over, I felt sufficiently interviewed.

Later I wondered about what the French taxpayers got for their money. They got to hit me, but I wasn't booked, jailed or deported. They paid the police and the hospital bills and I'm still angry. Perhaps they got their money's worth. They were hunting enemies that spring night, and they bought one for life.

Victorians carried market-baskets when they shopped. They also dressed for the occasion and kept each other company following specific rules of etiquette relating to their position and class.

18. Shoppers. *Carte de visite by Mrs. Moore, Canal Street, New York City, c. 1860s.*

19. BLACK COFFEE, TWO CENTS A CUP.
Unmounted photograph on collodion printing-out paper,
by Paul Géniaux, Halles Centrales, Paris, 1902.

20. LEEKS, BEAUTIFUL LEEKS. *Unmounted photograph by Paul Géniaux,
Halles Centrales, Paris, 1902.*

21. WATER CARRIER WITH HEAD STRAPS. *Carte de visite by Merille, Mexico City, c. 1860s.*

22. RAGPICKER. *Unmounted photograph on collodion printing-out paper by Paul Géniaux, Paris, 1902.*

The Victorians recycled and the ragpickers were their agents. In addition to rags, they scrapped bones, glass, metal, anything that could be reused.

In my opinion public education is overrated. It attempts to educate people against their wills and fails more than it succeeds. In other times, illiteracy was more public than education and street scribes were available to put words to paper and read letters received.

23. STREET SCRIBE. *Carte de visite by Giorgio Conrad, Naples, c. 1868.*

24. HOMELESS FAMILY. *Carte de visite by Giorgio Conrad, Naples, c. 1870.*

BEING homeless has to be experienced to be understood. You might think that food is more essential to life than shelter, but to experience a full measure of humiliation, terror and despair, you must go homeless and hungry. Being homeless cripples the spirit. It throws people off bridges and under trains. Other times it makes fast friends of strangers.

Willie and Jimmy and I walked the same streets of the Latin Quarter. Willie was seventeen and played the guitar. He hadn't yet decided what he was going to do if he was drafted. Jimmy still had an army haircut. He had left his base after receiving orders to go to Vietnam. A peace group had gotten him a new name and passport and a ticket to Paris. For a little while he and I shared a ten franc room. It was grim but it was off the street.

Teresa and Jimmy were friends. She was a fifteen-year-old runaway. She was too pretty and too young to be on the street. She was energetic and hustled men without being tactful or designing. My first impression of her was that she would end up in a brothel or a castle or both. I was walking with Jimmy one night when Teresa bolted from a cafe and joined us. She had just traded a large African man dinner for favors he would never receive. She had hurt his feelings and pride and he wasn't about to let the matter drop. For the rest of the night and into the early morning, we protected her from him. Moving around the quarter, we'd lose him temporarily and he would find us again. At one point we split up, with Jimmy falling back to confuse the pursuer. For a while Teresa and I tried to sleep on a bench by the Seine, but our wino neighbors wouldn't leave her alone. Everyone wanted Teresa. Finally, I convinced her unhappy suitor to call it an evening. I did so by mustering my craziest, sleep-deprived look and charging him. He ran off and returned with a larger African man who asked me not to hurt his friend. I quickly agreed and suggested that we all get some sleep. Three tired friends regrouped back at the ten franc room. She and Jimmy got the single bed and I drew the remaining floor space. Letting one arm fall off the bed, she held my hand till daybreak.

I saw Teresa later that day and she told me that a man was taking her to Switzerland. Then a few days later, Jimmy's new identity blew up for some forgotten reason and he had to leave Paris. Willie outlasted all of us. Afterwards I heard that he had gone to Canada and was living in a burned-out building. I hope they're all safe. The friendships you form when you are down and out are bittersweet. Each is an oasis. Likewise, you become attached to every place that shelters and turns you out, homeless again. However gentle the return, it leaves you crying in the street.

25. CHIMNEY SWEEPS. *Cabinet card, c. 1870.*

CHILD LABOR

CHILD labor was a fact of life in the nineteenth century. The apprentice system had initiated young laborers into the work force for centuries. Arising factories naturally allowed for a percentage of young employees. When I think of how bored I was in high school, going to work early doesn't seem like such a bad idea.

In the second half of the nineteenth century child labor abuses first received widely published attention in exposés and reports supported by a growing middle class. Underlying their charitable contents were expressions of class and ethnic intolerance. In London, 1877, the Society for Organizing Charitable Relief and Repressing Mendicity published a report on "The Employment of Italian Children for Mendicant and Immoral Purposes." Regarding immorality, its authors maintained that Italian girls were sooner liable to demoralization because they matured faster than English girls. Everyday reality was less sexy.

The influx of poor foreign populations into urban centers threatened cheap labor and brought on the uneasy clash of cultures. Their children went to work earlier and in greater numbers than did their industrialized counterparts.

Reformers saw evil in all child labor. Even the activities of the all-American newsboy were suspect. Seeking scandal everywhere, their zealous numbers naturally unearthed some real problems. The most notorious misuse of nineteenth-century child labor was by the padroni, who "bought" children from gullible impoverished parents. A small sum of money sealed each deal and it was promised that the child would receive musical or other instruction over a prescribed period of time. Typically, a padrone would oversee a group of children, like Dickens' Fagin. They would be sent out to work the streets, profiting their masters by playing music, selling candy or flowers, and otherwise generating income.

Padrone scandals fostered the belief that the poor were more sinful than their superiors. I suspect otherwise. Crimes against children ignore class lines. It is possible that child labor was good and bad in turns, and efforts to regulate it were both helpful and misdirected.

Today it is popular to think of the state as a parent protecting us from the cradle to the grave. In this scenario we are all helpless children. When that parent fails, the child had better take care of himself.

26. CONTAINERS. *Carte de visite by Giorgio Conrad, Naples, c. 1870.*

27. ORGAN BOY. *Carte de visite by
C. D. Fredericks, New York City, c. 1860s.
Gift of Henry Deeks.*

28. HARP BOY. *Carte de visite by
C. D. Fredericks, New York City, c. 1860s.*

29. HAWKER. *Cabinet card. Label reverse reads "Charles Parker 3-1-94, 19 Summer St., Rutland, Vt."*

30. SONG AND DANCE MEN. *Cabinet card, c. 1900. Vaudeville and the stage first played the streets.*

31. STREET DANCER. *Snapshot by Joseph E. Rhoads,* Vermont Life *photographer, c. 1920s.*

This street entertainer dances before a windup phonograph. Keeping pace with the changing technology of canned music, he anticipates buskers who carry portable amplifiers and taped music to work.

32. STREET PIANO OPERATORS AND A POLICEMAN. *Stereoview published by Kilburn Brothers, Littleton, New Hampshire, c. 1890.*

IN this 1890 stereoview, a policeman poses with the operators of a street piano, cat and mouse together. This card is a quaint amusement, but there was something felt at nineteenth century street level that we would all feel in time—the state's growing authority. As the world shrinks, the state's authority is ever more present. The poor grow in number and they are criminalized. How can our laws and borders hold them? For all the problems it faces, the state has achieved notable success in one area— the determined surveillance of the innocent.

Unless you've traveled without sufficient funds, you're not likely to know what I'm talking about. Twice I visited England without money, the first time to ask a friend to buy me a ticket back to the States. Unschooled in the ways of slipping past the customs cat, I told one plainly of my intentions. He replied that I was a threat to the English economy. I told him that I wasn't after any Brit's job, and then I told him what I thought of him. He closed his post, leaving me standing there, and after a while, someone escorted me to detention for the night.

The next day, I still had a little money, so I elected to fly to Holland. It was something that I could do without British permission. The Dutch also refused me entry, alerted by a British mark on my passport, but they had me sign an I.O.U. and board a plane for New York.

My second down and out attempt at visiting England was different from start to finish. I had a new passport and a hitchhiking partner carrying cash that she agreed to let me hold and present as my own. At customs, it appeared that I was passing muster, when the customs man began reading a love letter he found in my knapsack, tempted by its psychedelic borders. I wanted to see friends in London so I let this pass, thinking he looked for drug references amid the heartbreak.

Anyway, the mouse isn't supposed to beat the cat. The mouse wins by surviving. Just so, a person pursuing some meager livelihood on the street is obliged to study human nature and blend with his surroundings. The vagabond dreams of a world without borders. For now, I put aside other memories of problems with authority around borders and street corners. Apprehended once for busking, I demonstrated a crank organ to a moving paddy wagon full of curious French police, knowing we shared a rare passage, cat and mouse together.

33. THE ORGAN GRINDER'S MONKEY. *Snapshot by Grace D. Chipman, Boston, 4th of July, 1898.*

In 1973 I was driving a 1952 Cadillac limousine. It had belonged to a private girls' school, a Connecticut state senator and a Cadillac collector. I had watched its tires flatten slowly by the side of a country road before thinking to offer a hundred dollars for it. It was about to carry me cross-country by way of Long Island, where I knew an old-time organ grinder.

Al had been an organ grinder for forty years. He had started out selling patent medicines from the back of a Model T. He had used a monkey act then to draw a crowd. He made enough money in his early wanderings to buy an old hotel in Texas. As an organ grinder, he had worked in amusement parks and films, posed for ads, pursuing his specialty act with little competition. Everything I know about training monkeys I learned from Al in his kitchen, where he kept three monkeys in separate cages.

Sitting in this kitchen, I got to examine music machines, show business memorabilia and assorted animal tricks. After a while, we visited the new mobile home parked in his yard. A check had to be made out to the company that financed it and there were other monkeys to feed. When Al sat down to take care of this business, he began talking about his old medicine show days, repeating the patter that he once used to attract the curious. Many stories followed, spiked with hits off a whiskey bottle, and by the time the check was in an envelope and ready to mail, most of the afternoon had passed. Al put the envelope in his pocket and we walked to a nearby mailbox. There we discovered that it was missing. Retracing our steps, we were unable to find it. Inside his cage a young monkey pickpocket was tearing it apart. I spent the rest of that afternoon watching Al tape together the kind of computerized payment card that we were then routinely warned not to bend, fold or mutilate. The check to the finance company was repaired in the same manner, and I realized between shared hits of whiskey that I was witnessing as good a story as any he had told.

Repairmen made their rounds on foot not all that long ago. They made their presence known in the street below by a cry or a bell. Today you may cry for your life and not be heard.

34. TINKER. *Mounted collodion photograph from an anonymous amateur album, c. 1890s.*

35. SIDEWALK MISSIONARY. *Kodak No. 2 snapshot, c. 1892.*

MISSIONARIES were everywhere in the nineteenth century including urban sidewalks. Among them were earthly angels, idealistic, chaste young females determined to save souls as they found them. The good done by this type of person is still being done and I have sung and chanted for my supper to be in her presence. There are many people in need of help on the street and they attract varying amounts of charity and criticism, but sometimes charity is saintly and feminine.

When I was first on the street, my girlfriend would come and visit me, bringing money, and we would live like a normal couple, staying in hotels and eating in restaurants. At the end of one of these visits, there was so little money left over that she had only enough to get part way home from J.F.K., and I had only a bus ticket to take me from Orly to the edge of Paris.

It was late at night by the time I found an open door to a heated building entrance. I slept there in my sleeping bag until a screaming concierge woke me up around 5 a.m. and chased me from the building. I spent the rest of the night crying, writing a love letter on a park bench. When it got light, I walked to the center of the city to check for mail at American Express. Given my uncertain future, I welcomed the familiar visit to the mailroom. I had no mail, but as I walked away, I saw a woman seated off by herself, staring blankly at a letter. She looked so troubled that I asked her what was wrong. She said that she was waiting for money that hadn't arrived. She had lost her luggage and her hotel room and didn't know what to do. I remembered in an instant that I had the address of a young heiress who attended the same college as my girlfriend. She didn't like me, but I couldn't see her turning away a sister in distress.

As we walked to that address, my new acquaintance did most of the talking. She had gone to a good college and afterwards worked her way around the world as a model. Her missing trunk contained clothes, a facebook and make-up, the tools of her trade. She had managed to find an understudy part in the play *Hair* but hadn't gone on yet. She was ten years older than I was. Her talking helped me forget my own desperate situation.

We soon arrived at a large doorway that opened into a landscaped courtyard. The apartment we sought was nestled in one corner of the courtyard. Its door was answered not by a Yankee heiress but by a mousy American girl. The heiress was away until tomorrow. I quickly introduced myself and my companion and explained her situation. The mouse turned out to be a roommate, who was paying rent to sleep on a couch in the living room. Good-hearted and open, she invited us inside. I stayed for supper and my story-telling earned me an invitation to spend the night. The model was offered the other living room couch and I was given the one bedroom.

I took a long bath and got under the clean covers of a featherbed. I wondered about my improved sleeping accommodations just long enough to get comfortable, when the bedroom door opened and on switched a light. It was the heiress and a Frenchman. He must have thought that I was her steady, because he got very apologetic and started backing out the door. She got angry and wanted to know what I was doing in her bed. The mouse appeared in the doorway and was having a nervous breakdown. For my part, I was eyeing my clothes on a chair across the room, considering how I was going to find my way to an uncontested park bench. Into the center of this storm glided the model, who announced simply and clearly that I could share her couch. Once everyone else was safely in bed, she took me all-giving and quietly made love to me. The next morning a departing heiress made it clear, as she walked by our couch, that she wanted us both out of her apartment by noon. We did as she said, but first the model went out and bought some groceries and made us breakfast. Her generosity teased a selfish world—her money waited for her at American Express. I don't remember where I spent the next night or found my next meal, except that it wasn't with her. I saw her only once after that and she kissed me hello. We missed each other a couple of times at the theater where *Hair* was playing. There I made friends with her friends. Later she told me over the phone that she was moving to Brittany.

I became a regular at the theater, taking advantage of free seats reserved for friends of the cast. One of the actors became a close friend and ally. Thinking about it now, I saw so little of the model and she did so much for me, she must have been an angel.

36. ORGAN GRINDER AND TAMBOURINE GIRL. *Carte de visite by C. D. Fredericks, New York City, c. 1860s. Gift of Henry Deeks.*

903. PARIS
Halles Centrales
Le Père la Serrure   E. L. D.

37. KEYS CUT. *French post card, c. 1905.*

WHEN Americans think of French post cards, they usually think of the erotic ones smuggled home in steamer trunks at the beginning of the twentieth century. Those cards are indeed French, and fun to look at, but they are not of particular interest to collectors in their country of origin. They are more likely to prize a post card of a public character drawn from their rich social history. This class of post card was more successfully published in France than anywhere else in the world.

It was in the first decade of this century that post cards gained world-wide popularity. Renewed photographic printing processes and improved means of distribution delivered them everywhere. They were affordable images for the millions. It was only natural that post card photographers turned their cameras on the common man. In France the mix of art, liberty and beautiful streets inspired democratic expression. Its booming post card industry employed 200,000 people at its peak.

The French, however, were interested in cheap images of street workers long before post cards. They supported vendors hawking inexpensive prints of public characters and otherwise encouraged studies of the working poor. Alfred Franklin's *Dictionaire Historique des Arts, Metiers et Professions de Paris* informs us that fifty-eight individuals worked as water carriers in Paris in 1292. In 1701, the ragpickers' district was on rue Neuve-Saint Martin. In 1774, two maidens named Demoncy and Varechon circulated handbills advertising their service of giving dog and cat haircuts on the quai Pelletier for four sols per operation. The French history of the street can be that specific. The American experience is about energetic change and an uprooted, fluid, seeking population. A nostalgic interest in its poorer classes is not an essential Yankee notion. Just the same, America had its share of street workers.

Every nation represented by American immigrants contributed its own traditions and culture, including its own street workers. The predominant Anglo culture strongly influenced the peddlers, hawkers and street criers of early America. Later waves of nineteenth century immigration, notably around the time of the Civil War and between 1890 and 1920, had a different effect. The majority of these immigrants were from the poorer nations of southern and eastern Europe. Their street life was abundant, varied and hungry. Their immigration was allowed because America needed cheap labor. American workers were less enthusiastic about this new competition. The unwanted immigrants, particularly dark-skinned ones, were caricatured in the popular press according to street occupations: Italian organ grinders, Jewish ragmen and Gypsy tinkers exemplified their swarthy masses. Immigrant ghettos were born of that time and economics.

It's remarkable how few photographs document these people and their neighborhoods. In twenty years, I've looked at hundreds of thousands of American photographs taken before 1920 and I have seen less than 100 unpublished images of newly arrived Italians. My maternal grandparents emigrated to New York from Milan and Genoa around 1900 and our earliest family photographs date to just before the Depression. The poor had other priorities.

Photography in its first seven decades (1840–1910) was supported primarily by the upper and middle classes. War is democratic in that it depends upon the universal soldier and he posed for the photographer as did the occasional proud tradesman showing off the tools of his trade. There were millions of cartes de visite made during the 1860s and 70s and allowing for the drafted and the industrious, some were taken of poor people but few were taken for them. Cartes de visite sound inexpensive at 25 cents per dozen, a contemporary rate, but not when the going wage is three dollars a week. A working man didn't visit a friend's home, dropping a carte in an appointed silver tray, to be later placed in a fancy leather bound album. Not until around 1905 was a broader application of the photographic arts realized with post card producing cameras. They made photographs that could be developed ready to mail and posted for a couple of pennies or less. This was the true source of democratic photography. At last everyman was a subject.

38. HALLES CENTRALES. *French real photo post card by Photographie Paul, Paris, 1907.*
Photographer's assistant and sample work in background.

39. SWEEP. *"Bill Phillips 1904" by W. Ph. Weick, Chicago. Cabinet card.*

40. WIRE WALKER. *Real photo post card, U.S., c. 1915.*

41. GYPSY BEAR TRAINER. *Published photo post card, Rome, c. 1910.*

PLATE 41 represents a Gypsy bear trainer, his assistants and onlookers. The Gypsies were not the only street performers who were animal trainers, but this work suited the way they lived. Trained animals require a lot of attention and stroking. Since land-lords generally oppose tenants keeping bears in apartments and storefronts, Gypsy camps on the edge of town were better suited for this purpose. They were welcomed there as guard animals. Performing bears were among the first animals banned from city streets, where their association with Gypsies compromised their popularity.

Many people think of Gypsies as beggars and thieves. They are also thought of as mysterious, romantic wanderers, an image they've encouraged since they left India for forgotten reasons centuries ago. In their time they have been harassed, persecuted and mass-murdered. The authorities generally dislike Gypsies because they resist carrying identification and tend not to be home when trouble calls.

In the unlikely event that a band of Gypsies should visit your town, don't worry and don't leave anything of value out in the open. When approaching Gypsies for the first time, remember that you are more dangerous than they are. Their society is closed and surprisingly puritanical. They are illiterate by choice and their culture is rich in music, dance and storytelling. They were once respected for their knowledge of animals, especially horses, and were experts in the art of making older, worn-out ones appear younger. Yesterday's horse traders are today's used car salesmen and Gypsies made that transition particularly well in the United States. One other thing: if you ask a group of Gypsies to take you to their leader, you're broadcasting your ignorance. Theirs is a leaderless society. There are Gypsy kings, but no one has ordained them and they follow no lineage. They are self-appointed fools and loud-mouths. They are expected to host frequent parties and they are the first to be taken away when the police raid.

PARIS — Le Père FRANÇOIS, Marchand de Mouron

42. CHICKWEED SELLER. *French post card, c. 1905.*

FATHER François sells chickweed that he has harvested from a vacant lot. What he sells, in fact, is wild bird food. I use his post card to illustrate the often humble nature of street sellers. I have read of them selling everything from shoelaces to dog droppings. Matches were once commonly sold on the street and vendors of penny toys used to survive by their efforts. It's likely that merchants of this class relied as much on the sympathy of their public as on the value of their products. I can better explain this point from experience.

I was once so broke that the only thing of value that I had left to sell was the leather bomber jacket on my back. I made a sign advertising the coat for sale and stood in a public place. To my surprise, I survived the next three months by assuming this posture. I became a minor public character. I was offered food, places to stay and other things to sell. When I eventually sold the jacket for forty dollars, the buyer also gave me the leather jacket he was wearing. When I sold that one, I rushed to the flea market, bought a replacement and returned to my now familiar street corner.

Before the season for wearing jackets passed, I regained my self-confidence. My faith had been restored. I knew that whatever happened next, I would be provided for like a wild bird or the grass growing in the park.

43. SHOELACES. *French post card, Tours, c. 1905.*

44. SCARFS. *Carte de visite by Georges Sommer, Naples, c. 1870. Gift of Matthew Isenburg.*

47. AMBULANT PHOTOGRAPHER ON THE BANKS OF THE SEINE.
French real photo post card, c. 1920s.

48. THE KNIFE GRINDER. *French published photo post card, DL series, c. 1910.*

49. BILL STICKER. *Anonymous U.S. carte de visite, c. 1865.*

50. POLITICAL BILL STICKER. *French real photo post card, c. 1910. Supporters of Etienne Coullet.*

51. WALKING ADVERTISERS. *French post card, c. 1905.*

523. *Les petits métiers de la rue.*
Marchand de statuettes.

52. IMAGE SELLER. *French post card, Tours, c. 1905.*

54. VENDOR OF APPLE PRESERVES TAGGED. *Belgian post card,*
Ern. Thill, Bruxelles, Types Russes series, c. 1910.

I.D.

I'VE referred elsewhere to the long history of licensing and regulating street occupations. Badges, tags, and permits are relics of those procedures and I've been challenged and charmed to collect them. To a degree they legitimized the most humble pursuits. However, there is a disturbing side to this business of tagging people. Operating at street level puts one in a vulnerable position in relation to authority and everyone's the police. It carries expectations of being inspected, identified, judged, lectured and otherwise harassed. Special attention is paid to the underclasses. Ghettos provide one organizing principle, and the routine over-policing of the poor offers another.

We are distracted by notions of progress, yet radical urban changes have not banished poverty, crime or public health risks. The short view of history records varieties of unrest from delinquency to revolution and seeks to control them. In the long view human nature remains unchanged. Progress only temporarily bullies the street.

The city street is the trail of our distant past. It provides food and distraction and connects us to one another. We were once in awe of its riches and would do well to reclaim this innocent appreciation. I first walked that street for adventure, heartache and sanity. I've been there as a war refugee, in between places, lost and hopeless. I've listened to music, taken photographs and fed birds there. I've gone falling, hoping for someone to catch me. There's a lot in living that can lead a person to the street and it has a pull that makes it hard to leave, but your papers better be in order.

55. WHEELBARROW PORTER. *Carte de visite from the One Dollar Photograph Gallery, B. F. Howland, operator, San Francisco, c. 1880.*

103. ALGÉRIE — Tête de Fakir

56. FAKIR. *Algerian post card, c. 1905.*

57. WILD MAN OF TENNESSEE. *Cabinet card by Hurd & Delany, Dalton, Georgia, c. late 1880s.*

Religious teachers preach that there are many paths to salvation. In some religions this belief is taken more literally than in others. Fakirs are sometimes both beggars and holy men. They seek a union with God by publicly practicing a variety of ascetic acts. The union they seek is not the feel good variety of a Christian with perfect church attendance—it is the direct experience of the divine in everything. The trouble is that a brush with God can leave you mad as a hatter.

I first met Jonas on his park bench in Paris. He had fiery red unkempt hair and a full beard. The soles of his shoes had holes and he slept outdoors. He claimed that until recently he had shared a student room with a baroness, who kicked him out because he gave her the crabs. He also claimed that he had worked as a nuclear physicist at the Enrico Fermi Institute and that a colleague hostile to his politics and religion had locked him in a cyclotron and turned on the juice. He claimed many things that seemed no less fantastic, including having a quarter million dollars in a New York bank account, but he made these claims with such creative force and energy that I mistook them for poetry and left it at that.

I followed Jonas around for a while impressed by his verbal wanderings and assaults. He had a way of encountering seemingly mild mannered strangers and rendering them homicidal in a few sentences. Other times he was less annoying, but always with a rapid-fire intensity. He was occasionally offered money, which he refused without explanation. When a telegram called me away to London, he offered to buy me a ticket. Surprised, I didn't say yes or no right away and he withdrew the offer.

Sometime later I returned to Paris but I couldn't find him. By an odd coincidence, I met an old college classmate of his in an English bookstore. He verified the more incredible details of our friend's life and had a chapter to add to the story.

Jonas had had a problem with the law. He had gone to a bank that refused to give him money from his infamous account, so he threw a chair through a window. When the police arrested him, he had $1000 in cash backing one shoe hole and $1000 in traveler's checks in the other. His wife's lawyer had tied up the rest of his funds. He was taken to a psychiatric hospital.

I followed directions there, but once inside, I couldn't tell the staff from the patients. I was sent in different directions. I left frustrated. Maybe these words will complete that visit. I hope it got better, Jonas. You were mad, but you were inspired—the chair through the bank window proved that.

58. CARTS AND CARS. *French press photo of Marseille murder scene, 1934.*

PROBLEMS WITH CARS

Looking at a nineteenth century city street in a photograph, I first notice the open space. There is a buggy here and there and perhaps a delivery wagon. It is casually crossed on foot and its buildings permit sunlight. I know that automobiles will soon crowd this street in the name of progress. They will disrupt family and community life and inspire suburbs and malls.

I can't reconcile cars and street life, but I believe that there's a force more deliberate than ourselves that nurtures neighborhoods. Streets will empty of cars and fill with people again as the population grows and our transportation machinery moves above and below us. Humble workers may or may not be welcomed on the unknown streets of the future, but they will be there.

At some point well into my adult life, I came to the dramatic realization that all my youthful influences, all my guides, had been either stoned, drunk, crazy or otherwise lost. This thought was hard-hitting and left me feeling out-on-a-limb, so I looked for leadership elsewhere. New teachers carried me forward, but it took less time to appreciate their limitations and less time to fire them. I am left with one persistent thought, namely that I don't need gurus or priests, philosophers, politicians, policemen or generals to tell me the difference between right and wrong. My heart knows the difference.

I fear for the moment that my single-minded pursuit of street life may be more excessive than heartfelt. Specialists worry me. They remind me of the fabled blindmen, who in describing different parts of an elephant, described different animals. I was once interviewed by a court psychologist following a cautiously theatrical confrontation with a skid row cop who beat up bums. The court had been misinformed that I was homeless. When I told its representative that I was just following my inner voice, he wrote down in his official report that I heard voices. People, in my experience, don't fit so easily into boxes.

Love has a language of its own. It exists without our permission and beyond our control. How much other apparent chaos serves a higher purpose? The media informs us that loners are assassins, but even the most pitiful madman may have been so humbled by a prophet's dream.

KEN APPOLLO
PARIS, 1993

NOTES

FRONTISPIECE. A wayside scene. Stereoview with London Stereoscopic Company blindstamp. Montgomery's "Lines on an Organ Boy" printed reverse, late 1850s.

INTRODUCTION. The young mechanic. Carte de visite by Gustav Mittweida, Germany, 1880s.

Old shoes. Carte de visite by Roberto Rive, Naples, c. 1870.

2. THE WALKING AGENT. Henry Leonard (1812–89) worked as an agent for Heidelberg College of Tiffin, Ohio. He began this career after successfully pursuing his own business interests for twenty-eight years. In May of 1856, the Board of Trustees of Heidelberg College voted him their financial agent. Accepting their selection as a calling, he sold his business to his brother and informed his wife and family that he would be spending long periods of time away from home. He was then forty-four years of age. In the next thirty-one years of his life he traveled 108,245 miles raising money for the College. Much of this distance was covered on foot, sometimes hitching rides on passing wagons and stages. His main purpose in traveling as he did was to limit his expenses, making more money available to the College. In his first twenty-three years, his traveling expenses totaled only $2380.71. He retired his agency poorer than he began it.

Leonard's old business instincts served him well as he pioneered advertising and self-promotional uses of photography. His carte de visite is one of a series of theatrically posed photographs taken in the late 1860s. In 1871, he mailed over 9000 of these to prospective donors. Each mailing included Leonard's self-addressed envelope with a request for a voluntary contribution or the return of the portraits.*

*E. I. F. Williams, *Heidelberg*, The Banta Publishing Company, Menosha, Wisconsin, 1952, Chapter IX, "The Fisherman," pp. 113–129.

3. THE OLD LEATHERMAN. Jules Bourglay walked the same 365 miles every thirty-four days between Connecticut and New York. He wore a suit made of hand sewn leather fragments that weighed sixty pounds. He began his eccentric walk in 1859, an escaped lunatic fleeing a French madhouse and painful memories of financial ruin and lost love. He rarely spoke, ate when offered food, slept outdoors, and died in a cave near Sing Sing, New York, in 1889. Anonymous cabinet card, c. 1880s.

16. Closing vignette. A protester arrested. Detail of French postcard by N. D. Phot, May 1, 1906.

21. WATER CARRIER WITH HEAD STRAPS.

For most of the nineteenth century it took far more effort than just turning on a tap to keep clean. It involved hauling in water, perhaps a quarter of a mile or more, and carrying it, perhaps, up several flights of stairs. It is easy to dismiss this as a minor inconvenience; even Octavia Hill, the eminent housing reformer, who ought to have known better, thought that a water supply on each floor of a large tenement block was unnecessary. Yet, for most labourers' families, lack of running water meant queuing up at the local street pump or tap, in foul weather as well as fine, carrying heavy pails through muddy and uneven streets and courtyards, an endless round of drudgery, day in, day out. Perhaps, like filth and noise, smells and overcrowding, the poor got used to it, although no doubt children would grumble when given the task. Even if it was simply yet another of the many accepted chores of working-class life, it was one which acted as a deterrent to cleanliness and thus to health.*

Indoor plumbing eliminated the need for water porters and created a demand for plumbers.

*Anthony S. Wohl, *Endangered Lives*, Methuen, London, 1983, pp. 61–62.

32. STREET PIANO OPERATORS AND A POLICEMAN. The street piano, first popularized in the 1890s, was commonly known as a hurdy gurdy, a misnomer. The real hurdy gurdy, a semi-mechanical fiddle, was one of the first two European applications of the crank, imported from China by Marco Polo; the other was the coffee mill.

33. ORGAN GRINDER'S MONKEY. The modern American view of an organ grinder is that of an Italian with a mustache, bandanna and monkey, a creation of the popular press and Hollywood. A nineteenth century eyewitness describes a more varied procession:

> . . . . big organs drawn by a donkey, and little organs carried by boys; nondescript boxes with a cradle at the top and two babies drawn by a woman; uprights on a stick with a little handle, turned by a crazy old man; chests open in front and shut at the back, or shut in the front and open at the back. There are flute organs, with a wonderful system of wooden pipes, visible through glass; great magnified accordians, played somehow with a handle—horrid things, which grind only the Old Hundredth and a chant on metal pipes. There are tinkling cupboards which remind one of Dickens' piano-forte with the works taken out, so irregular and uncertain is the effect of the handle upon the tune. There are illustrated organs, with Chinese Mandarins performing conjuring tricks in a row, or Nebuchadnezzar's band; and there are organs with a monkey, triangle, bones, tambourine or whistle obligato.*

*Rev. H. R. Haweis, *Music and Morals*, Harper and Brothers Publishers, New York, 1871, p. 458.

38. HALLES CENTRALES. It was the wholesale farmer's market in Paris. When it was moved out of the city in the early 1970s, it was replaced first by a large hole and later by Pompidou Center and a square, both popular attractions. The resulting loss of tradition and culture was protested, but working class Paris didn't count for much in the city's architects' plans.

When I was first down and out in Paris, a predawn visit to this market sometimes provided casual labor and there was always something to eat. Halles Centrales was the glorious setting for the movie *Irma La Douce* (1963) starring Shirley MacLaine and Jack Lemmon.

39. SWEEP. Crossing sweeps used to keep their part of the street clean, depending upon tips from grateful pedestrians. Their fundraising approach was not unlike that of the people who clean your windshield in stopped traffic, only more passive. The cautious demeanor of nineteenth century street workers was an understandable reaction to strictly enforced vagrancy laws. The most meager living outdoors was preferable to a month in the workhouse. Today's street sweepers, where they are found, are municipal employees with wages and benefits.

40. WIRE WALKER. Solitary showmen are part of an ancient entertainment tradition. They banded together to form the first circuses.

47. AMBULANT PHOTOGRAPHER. Earlier photo artists who traveled from place to place did so mostly in large vans drawn by oxen. The modern street photographer favors Polaroid cameras.

54. VENDOR TAGGED. For a charming account of how newsboys in the first part of the twentieth century resisted wearing badges, read David Nason's *Children of the City*, Anchor Press, Garden City, New York, 1985, pp. 150-1

55. WHEELBARROW PORTER. Today much is driven that used to be carried, a change that has crowded streets and eliminated jobs. The porter, a man who works with his back, is the most diminished of the old street occupations. We forget that if we had to, we could carry our cities ourselves.

ACKNOWLEDGEMENTS

I'm grateful to the strangers and friends who helped me when I was down and out in Paris, among them Kavi Alexander, Jill Beede, Sara Matthews, Charlene McKoin and Michele Shulterbrandt. Phillipe and Chantelle Rothan visited me at the police hospital and smuggled in whiskey and Kenneth Patchen. Rob Gelblum provided ongoing support, street music and careful editing.

I am profoundly in debt to Harold Bradford, who showed me how to survive off the road and whose junk shop was my college sanctuary and the model for my first business.

Michele loaned me the money to buy my first crank organ from Vicki Glasgow, who referred me to Bill Scolnik and Rick Tomita to learn about its care, repair and replacement. Joel and Kate Kopp of America Hurrah Antiques freely provided early photography lessons and loaned me the money to buy my second music machine. More recently, Joel helped edit and focus this book.

The "Living with Monkeys" story was inspired by Al Seigle.

I completed my first manuscript, *Organ Grinder*, in 1972. Deborah Addis told me how bad it was and saved it from being another term paper. Wesleyan University professors and staff tolerated and supported this project in its infancy and Elizabeth Swain, the college archivist, has been especially helpful over the years.

I am also grateful for those who provided inspirational places to write, to John Hartung and Rosamund Pittman, Sande Green and staff of the Hotel des Grandes Ècoles.

I would like to thank Jackie Huey for responding to my *New York Times* "Author's Query" and for daring me to go to China.

I was helped and encouraged by everyone who read, edited or otherwise responded to the manuscript in its various forms, especially Susan Appollo, Beth Bailey, Robert Blake, Sara and Stanley Burns, Marjorie Clisson, Matthew and Barbara Isenburg, dede Kirby, Joan Kraft, May Lum, Christine Martino, Susan Quasha, Françoise Reynaud, Marylyn Rosenblum and John Wood.

I am grateful to friends and associates in the subculture of collectors and dealers, who helped me build my collection. In Paris, Françoise Doerr and Brigette and Marc Pagneux were excellent sources for beautiful photographs and Marc and Irène Lefebvre shared their expert knowledge of French postcards.

Carl Brandt and Susan Perlman shaped the book contract and made it author-friendly. Dennis Waters provided superior copywork. Matthew Isenburg generously assisted on the computer, as did May Lum and John Zanetich.

However, it has been in the design and production of this book that I have been most encouraged and uplifted. Carl Mautz promised to publish this book down the years and Cathie Leavitt, Rosemarie Mossinger and designer Richard Moore are the skilled and talented people who helped him keep that promise.

N n

Newcastle Salmon,
Delicate Salmon.

O o

OARS, or Sculler;
have a boat?

P p

Potatoes, two pounds
for a penny.

Q q

Quack Doctors vend
variety of medicines.

R r

Rabbit ho! rabbit,
fine fat Rabbit.

S ſ

Sweep foot ho!
ſweep for your foot!